CHRIST UPON THE WATERS

John Henry Newman

1899

CATHOLIC TRUTH SOCIETY

PUBLISHERS TO THE HOLY SEE

Cardinal Newman (1801-1890) was a giant of nineteenth century theology. He was beatified in 2010.

CTS ONEFIFTIES

First published 1857, in *Sermons Preached on Various Occasions*;
CTS edition, 1899.
Published by The Incorporated Catholic Truth Society,
40-46 Harleyford Road, London SE11 5AY
www.ctsbooks.org
All rights reserved.
Copyright © 2017 The Incorporated Catholic Truth Society.
ISBN 978 1 78469 529 3

Fear not, therefore, dear brethren of the household of faith, any trouble that may come upon us… Doubt not that He will appear to rescue you.

CHRIST UPON THE WATERS

A SERMON
JOHN HENRY NEWMAN, D.D.[1]

Navicula autem in medio mari jactabatur fluctibus; erat enim contrarius ventus. Quartâ autem vigiliâ noctis, venit ad eos ambulans super mare. Et videntes eum super mare ambulantem, turbati sunt, dicentes, Quia phantasma est. Et præ timore clamaverunt. Statimque Jesus locutus est eis, dicens, Habete fiduciam; ego sum; nolite timere.—EVANG. SEC. MATT., *c.* xiv. *v.* 24–27.

The boat in the midst of the sea was tossed with the waves; for the wind was contrary. And in the fourth watch of the night He came to them, walking upon the sea. And they, seeing Him walking upon the sea, were troubled, saying, It is an apparition. And they cried out for fear. And immediately Jesus spoke to them, saying, Be of good heart; it is I; fear ye not.

---

[1] Preached on October 27, 1850, in St. Chad's, Birmingham, at the Installation of the Right Rev. Dr. Ullathorne, First Bishop of the See. Reprinted by permission from Cardinal Newman's *Sermons Preached on Various Occasions* (Longmans).

The earth is full of the marvels of divine power; "Day to day uttereth speech, and night to night showeth knowledge." The tokens of Omnipotence are all around us, in the world of matter, and in the world of man: in the dispensation of nature, and in the dispensation of grace. To do impossibilities, I may say, is the prerogative of Him, who made all things out of nothing, who foresees all events before they occur, and controls all wills without compelling them. In emblem of this His glorious attribute, He came to His disciples in the passage I have read to you walking upon the sea—the emblem or hieroglyphic among the ancients of the impossible; to show them that what is impossible with man is possible with God. He who could walk the waters could also ride triumphantly upon what is still more fickle, unstable, tumultuous, treacherous—the billows of human wills, human purposes, human hearts. The bark of Peter was struggling with the waves, and made no progress; Christ came to him walking upon them; He entered the boat, and by entering it He sustained it. He did not abandon Himself to it, but He brought it near to Himself; He did not merely take refuge in it, but He made Himself the strength of it and the pledge and cause of a successful passage. "Presently," another gospel says, "the ship was at the land whither they were going."

Such was the power of the Son of God, the Saviour of man, manifested by visible tokens in the material world when He came upon earth; and such, too, it has ever since signally shown itself to be, in the history of that mystical ark which He then formed to float upon the ocean of human opinion. He told His chosen servants to form an ark for the salvation of souls; He gave them directions how to construct it,—the length, breadth, and height, its cabins and its windows; and the world, as it gazed upon it, forthwith began to criticize. It pronounced it framed quite contrary to the scientific rules of shipbuilding; it prophesied, as it still prophesies, that such a craft was not sea-worthy; that it was not water-tight; that it would not float; that it would go to pieces and founder. And why it does not, who can say, except that the Lord is in it? Who can say why so old a framework, put together eighteen hundred years ago, should have lasted, against all human calculation, even to this day; always going, and never gone; ever failing, yet ever managing to explore new seas and foreign coasts—except that He, who once said to the rowers, "It is I, be not afraid," and to the waters, "Peace," is still in His own ark which He has made, to direct and to prosper her course?

And hence so many instances are to be found in history, of the triumph of the bark of Peter amid adversity of every kind. "The floods have lifted up, the floods have lifted up their voice; the floods have lifted up their waves with the noise of many waters. Wonderful are the surges of the sea; wonderful is the Lord on high." It is the Lord from heaven, who is our light in the gloom, our confidence in the storm. There is nothing hard to Him who is almighty; nothing strange to Him who is all-manifold in operation and all-fruitful in resource. The clouds break, and the sun shines, and the sea is smooth, in its appointed season. Such, my dear Brethren, is the thought which naturally possesses the mind on a day like this, when we are met together solemnly to return thanks to our merciful God for the restoration of the Catholic Hierarchy to the faithful of this land. His works are ever slow and gradual; year after year brings its silent influence and contribution in aid of the object which He may have in view; and we are unable, except artificially and for convenience, to divide into portions or stages what with Him is the continuous introduction of an integral whole. But still from time to time occur greater and more striking events, in which the past and the future are, as it were, summed up; and which, though intrinsically great, may be taken as symbols and are representatives of even more than they are themselves, of the labours and the prospects of a course of years. And such as this is the great act which we are now commemorating: it witnesses that much has been done; it predicts that much is to follow: it is the authoritative recognition and seal of the successes which God has given us, and the instrument of their consolidation. Well then may we rejoice on this day; and happily does it fall on the feast of Our Lady's Patronage, for to whom, under God, are our acknowledgments more truly due, and our expectations more securely turned, than to His all-holy and ever-glorious Mother?

Time was, my Brethren, when the forefathers of our race were a savage tribe, inhabiting a wild district beyond the limits of this quarter of the earth. Whatever brought them thither, they had no local attachments there or political settlement; they were a restless people, and whether urged forward by enemies or by desire of plunder, they left their place, and passing through the defiles of the mountains on the frontiers of Asia, they invaded Europe, setting out on a journey towards the farther west. Generation after generation passed away; and still this fierce and haughty race moved forward. On, on they went; but travel availed them not; the change of place could bring them no truth, or peace, or hope, or stability of heart; they could not flee from themselves. They carried with them their superstitions and their sins, their gods of iron and of clay, their savage sacrifices, their lawless witchcrafts, their hatred of their kind, and their ignorance of their destiny. At length they buried themselves in the deep forests of Germany, and gave themselves up to indolent repose; but they had not found their rest; they were still heathens, making the fair trees, the primeval work of God, and the innocent beasts of the chase, the objects and the instruments of their idolatrous worship. And, last of all, they crossed over the strait and made themselves masters of this island, and gave their very name to it; so that, whereas it had hitherto been called Britain, the southern part, which was their main seat, obtained the name of England. And now they had proceeded forward nearly as far as they could go, unless they were prepared to look across the great ocean, and anticipate the discovery of the world which lies beyond it.

What, then, was to happen to this restless race, which had sought for happiness and peace across the globe, and had not found it? Was it to grow old in its place, and dwindle away, and consume in the fever of its own heart, which admitted no remedy? or was it to become great by being overcome, and to enjoy the only real life of man, and rise to his only true dignity, by being subjected to a Master's yoke? Did its Maker and Lord see any good thing in it, of which, under His divine nurture, profit might come to His elect, and glory to His Name? He looked upon it, and He saw nothing there to claim any visitation of His grace, or to merit any relaxation of the awful penalty which its lawlessness and impiety had incurred. It was a proud race, which feared neither God nor man—a race ambitious, self-willed, obstinate, and hard of belief, which would dare everything, even the eternal pit, if it was challenged to do so. I say, there was nothing there of a nature to reverse the destiny which His righteous decrees have assigned to those who sin wilfully and despise Him. But the Almighty Lover of souls looked once again; and He saw in that poor, forlorn, and ruined nature, which He had in the beginning filled with grace and light, He saw in it, not what merited His favour, not what would adequately respond to His influences, not what was a necessary instrument of His purposes, but what would illustrate and preach abroad His grace, if He took pity on it. He saw in it a natural nobleness, a simplicity, a frankness of character, a love of truth, a zeal for justice, an indignation at wrong, an admiration of purity, a reverence for law, a keen appreciation of the beautifulness and majesty of order, nay, further, a tenderness and an affectionateness of heart, which He knew would become the glorious instruments of

His high will, when illuminated and vivified by His supernatural gifts. And so He who, did it so please Him, could raise up children to Abraham out of the very stones of the earth, nevertheless determined in this instance in His free mercy to unite what was beautiful in nature with what was radiant in grace; and, as if those poor Anglo-Saxons had been too fair to be heathen, therefore did he rescue them from the devil's service and the devil's doom, and bring them into the house of His holiness and the mountain of His rest.

It is an old story and a familiar, and I need not go through it. I need not tell you, my Brethren, how suddenly the word of truth came to our ancestors in this island and subdued them to its gentle rule; how the grace of God fell on them, and, without compulsion, as the historian tells us, the multitude became Christian; how, when all was tempestuous, and hopeless, and dark, Christ like a vision of glory came walking to them on the waves of the sea. Then suddenly there was a great calm; a change came over the pagan people in that quarter of the country where the gospel was first preached to them; and from thence the blessed influence went forth, it was poured out over the whole land, till one and all the Anglo-Saxon people were converted by it. In a hundred years the work was done; the idols, the sacrifices, the mummeries of paganism flitted away and were not, and the pure doctrine and heavenly worship of the Cross were found in their stead. The fair form of Christianity rose up and grew and expanded like a beautiful pageant from north to south; it was majestic, it was solemn, it was bright, it was beautiful and pleasant, it was soothing to the griefs, it was indulgent to the hopes of man; it was at once a teaching and a worship; it had a dogma, a mystery, a ritual of its own; it had an hierarchical form. A brotherhood of holy pastors, with mitre and crosier and uplifted hand, walked forth and blessed and ruled a joyful people. The crucifix headed the procession, and simple monks were there with hearts in prayer, and sweet chants resounded, and the holy Latin tóngue was heard, and boys came forth in white, swinging censers, and the fragrant cloud arose, and mass was sung, and the saints were invoked; and day after day, and in the still night, and over the woody hills and in the quiet plains, as constantly as sun and moon and stars go forth in heaven, so regular and solemn was the stately march of blessed services on earth, high festival, and gorgeous procession, and soothing dirge, and passing bell, and the familiar evening call to prayer: till he who recollected the old pagan time, would think it all unreal that he beheld and heard, and would conclude he did but see a vision, so marvellously was heaven let down upon earth, so triumphantly were chased away the fiends of darkness to their prison below.

Such was the change which came over our forefathers; such was the Religion bestowed upon them, bestowed on them as a second grant, after the grant of the territory itself; nay, it might almost have seemed as the divine guarantee or pledge of its occupation. And you know its name; there can be no mistake, my Brethren; you know what that Religion was called. It was called by no modern name—for modern religions then were not. You know, my dear Brethren, *what* religion has priests and sacrifices, and mystical rites, and the monastic rule, and care for the souls of the dead, and the profession of an ancient faith, coming through all ages from the Apostles. There is one, and only one, religion such: it is known everywhere; every poor boy in the street knows the name of it; there never was a time, since it first was, that its name was not known, and known to the multitude. It is called *Catholicism*—a worldwide name, and incommunicable; attached to us from the first; accorded to us by our enemies; in vain attempted, never stolen from us, by our rivals. Such was the worship which the English people gained when they emerged out of paganism into gospel light. In the history of their conversion, Christianity and Catholicity are one; they are, as in their own nature, so in that history, convertible terms. It was the Catholic faith which that vigorous young race heard and embraced,—that faith which is still found, the further you trace back towards the age of the Apostles, which is still visible in the dim distance of the earliest antiquity, and to which the witness of the Church, when investigated even in her first startings and simplest rudiments, "sayeth not the contrary." Such was the religion of the noble English; they knew not heresy; and, as time went on, the work did but sink deeper and deeper into their nature, into their social structure and their political institutions; it grew with their growth, and strengthened with their strength, till a sight was seen,—one of the most beautiful which ever has been given to man to see,— what was great in the natural order, made greater by its elevation into the supernatural. The two seemed as if made for each other; that natural temperament and that gift of grace; what was heroic, or generous, or magnanimous in nature, found its corresponding place or office in the divine kingdom. Angels in heaven rejoiced to see the divinely wrought piety and sanctity of penitent sinners: Apostles, Popes, and Bishops, long since taken to glory, threw their crowns in transport at the foot of the throne, as saints, and confessors, and martyrs, came forth before their wondering eyes out of a horde of heathen robbers; guardian spirits no longer sighed over the disparity and contrast which had so fearfully intervened between themselves and the souls given to them in charge. It did indeed become a peculiar, special people, with a character and genius of its own; I will say a bold thing—in its staidness, sagacity, and simplicity, more like the mind that rules, through all time, the princely line of Roman pontiffs, than perhaps any other Christian people whom the world has seen. And so things went on for many centuries. Generation followed generation; revolution came after revolution; great men rose and fell: there were bloody wars, and invasions, conquests, changes of dynasty, slavery, recoveries, civil dissensions, settlements; Dane and Norman overran the land; yet all along Christ was upon the waters; and if they rose in fury, yet at His word they fell again and were in calm. The bark of Peter was still the refuge of the tempest-tost, and ever solaced and recruited those whom it rescued from the deep.

But at length a change again came over the land: a thousand years had well-nigh rolled, and this great people grew tired of the heavenly stranger who sojourned among them. They had had enough of blessings and absolutions, enough of the intercession of saints, enough of the grace of the sacraments, enough of the prospect of the next life. They thought it best to secure this life in the first place, because they were in possession of it, and then to go on to the next, if time and means allowed. And they saw that to labour for the next world was possibly to lose this; whereas, to labour for this world might be, for what they knew, the way to labour for the next also. Anyhow, they would pursue a temporal end, and they would account any one their enemy who stood in the way of their pursuing it. It was a madness; but madmen are strong, and madmen are clever; so with the sword and the halter, and by mutilation and fine and imprisonment, they cut off, or frightened away from the land, as Israel did in the time of old, the ministers of the Most High, and their ministrations: they "altogether broke the yoke, and burst the bonds." "They beat one, and killed another, and another they stoned," and at length they altogether cast out the Heir from His vineyard, and killed Him, "that the inheritance might be theirs." And as for the remnant of His servants whom they left, they drove them into corners and holes of the earth, and there they bade them die out; and then they rejoiced and sent gifts either to other, and made merry, because they had rid themselves of those "who had tormented them that dwelt upon the earth." And so they turned to enjoy this world, and to gain for themselves a name among men, and it was given unto them according to their wish. They preferred the heathen virtues of their original nature, to the robe of grace which God had given them: they fell back, with closed affections, and haughty reserve, and dreariness within, upon their worldly integrity, honour, energy, prudence, and perseverance; they made the most of the natural man, and they "received their reward." Forthwith they began to rise to a station higher than the heathen Roman, and have, in three centuries, attained a wider range of sovereignty; and now they look down in contempt on what they were, and upon the Religion which reclaimed them from paganism.

Yes, my dear Brethren, such was the temptation of the evil one, such the fall of his victim, such the disposition of the Most High. The tempter said, "All these will I give thee, if, falling down, thou wilt adore me"; and their rightful Lord and Sovereign permitted the boast to be fulfilled. He permitted it for His greater glory: He might have hindered it, as He might hinder all evil; but He saw good, He saw it best, to let things take their course. He did not interfere, He kept silence, He retired from the land which would be rid of Him. And there were those at that crisis who understood not His providence, and would have interfered in His behalf with a high hand. Holy men and true they were, zealous for God, and tender towards His sheep; but they divined not His will. It was His will to leave the issue to time, and to bring things round slowly and without violence, and to conquer by means of His adversaries. He willed it that their pride should be its own correction; that they should be broken without hands, and dissolve under their own insufficiency. He who might have brought myriads of Angels to the rescue, He who might have armed and blessed the forces of Christendom against His persecutors, wrought more wondrously. He deigned not to use the carnal weapon: He bade the drawn sword return to its shèath: He refused the combinations and the armaments of earthly kings. He who sees the end from the beginning, who is "justified in His words, and overcomes when He is judged," did but wait. He waited patiently; He left the world to itself, nor avenged His Church, but stayed till the fourth watch of the night, when His faithful sons had given up hope, and thought His mercy towards them at an end. He let the winds and the waves insult Him and His own; He suffered meekly the jeers and blasphemies which rose on every side, and pronounced the downfall of His work. "All things have an end," men said; "there is a time for all things; a time to be born, and a time to die. All things have their course and their term; they may last a long time, but after all, a period they have, and not an immortality. So is it with man himself; even Mathusala and Noe exhausted the full fountain of their being, and the pitcher was at length crushed, and the wheel broken. So is it with nations; they rise, and they flourish, and they fall; there is an element in them, as in individuals, which wears out and perishes. However great they may be in their day, at length the moment comes, when they have attained their greatest elevation, and accomplished their full range, and fulfilled their scope. So is it with great ideas and their manifestations; they are realized, they prevail, and they perish. As the constituents of the animal frame at length refuse to hold together, so nations, philosophies, and religions one day lose their unity and undergo the common law of decomposition. Our nation doubtless will find its term at length, as well as others, though not yet; but that ancient faith of ours has come to nought already. We have nothing then to fear from the past; the past is not, the past cannot revive; the dead tell no tales; the grave cannot open. New adversaries we may have, but with the Old Religion we have parted once for all."

Thus speaks the world, deeming Christ's patience to be feebleness, and His loving affection to be enmity. And the faithful, on the other hand, have had their own misgivings too, whether Catholicism could ever flourish in this country again. Has it yet happened anywhere in the history of the Church, that a people which once lost its faith ever regained it? It is a gift of grace, a special mercy to receive it once, and not to be expected a second time. Many nations have never had it at all; from some it has been taken away, apparently without their fault, nay, in spite of their meritorious use of it. So was it with the old Persian Church, which, after enduring two frightful persecutions, had scarcely emerged from the second, when it was irretrievably corrupted by heresy. So was it with the famous Church of Africa, whose great saint and doctor's dying moments were embittered by the ravages around him of those fierce barbarians who were destined to be its ruin. What are we better than they? It is then surely against the order of Providence hitherto, that the gift once given should be given again; the world and the Church bear a concordant testimony here.

And the just Judge of man made as though He would do what man anticipated. He retired, as I have said, from the field; He yielded the battle to the enemy;—but He did so that He might in the event more signally triumph. He interfered not for near three hundred years, that His enemies might try their powers of mind in forming a religion instead of His own. He gave them three hundred years' start, bidding them to do something better than He, or something at all, if so be they were able, and He put Himself to every disadvantage. He suffered the daily sacrifice to be suspended, the hierarchy to be driven out, education to be prohibited, religious houses to be plundered and suppressed, cathedrals to be desecrated, shrines to be rifled, religious rites and duties to be interdicted by the law of the land. He would owe the world nothing in that revival of the Church which was to follow. He wrought, as in the old time by His prophet Elias, who, when he was to light the sacrifice with fire from heaven, drenched the burnt-offering with water the first time, the second time, and the third time; "and the water ran round about the altar, and the trench was filled up with water." He wrought as He Himself had done in the raising of Lazarus; for when He heard that His friend was sick, "He remained in the same place two days": on the third day He "said plainly, Lazarus is dead, and I am glad, for your sake, that I was not there, that you may believe;" and then, at length, He went and raised him from the grave. So too was it in His own resurrection; He did not rise from the Cross; He did not rise from His mother's arms; He rose from the grave, and on the third day.

So, my dear Brethren, is it now; "He hath taken us, and He will heal us; He will strike, and He will cure us. He will revive us after two days; on the third day He will raise us up, and we shall live in His sight." Three ages have passed away; the bell has tolled once, and twice, and thrice; the intercession of the saints has had effect; the mystery of Providence is unravelled; the destined hour is come. And, as when Christ arose, men knew not of His rising, for He rose at midnight and in silence, so when His mercy would do His new work among us, He wrought secretly, and was risen ere men dreamed of it. He sent not His Apostles and preachers, as at the first, from the city where He has fixed His throne. His few and scattered priests were about their own work, watching their flocks by night, with little time to attend to the souls of the wandering multitudes around them, and with no thoughts of the conversion of the country. But He came as a spirit upon the waters; He walked to and fro Himself over that dark and troubled deep; and wonderful to behold, and inexplicable to man, hearts were stirred, and eyes were raised in hope, and feet began to move towards the Great Mother, who had almost given up the thought and the seeking of them. First one, and then another, sought the rest which she alone could give. A first, and a second, and a third, and a fourth, each in his turn, as grace inspired him,—not altogether, as by some party understanding or political call,—but each drawn by divine power, and against his will, for he was happy where he was, yet with his will, for he was lovingly subdued by the sweet mysterious influence which called him on. One by one, little noticed at the moment, silently, swiftly, and abundantly, they drifted in till all could see at length that surely the stone was rolled away, and that Christ was risen and abroad. And as He rose from the grave, strong and glorious, as if refreshed with His sleep, so, when the prison doors were opened, the Church came forth, not changed in aspect or in voice, as calm and keen, as vigorous and as well furnished, as when they closed on her. It is told in legends, my Brethren, of that great saint and instrument of God, St. Athanasius, how that when the apostate Julian had come to his end, and persecution with him, the saintly confessor, who had been a wanderer over the earth, was found to the surprise of his people in his cathedral at Alexandria, seated on his episcopal throne, and clad in the vestments of religion. So it is now; the Church is coming out of prison as collected in her teaching, as precise in her action, as when she went into it. She comes out with pallium, and cope, and chasuble, and stole, and wonder-working relics, and holy images. Her bishops are again in their chairs, and her priests sit round, and the perfect vision of a majestic hierarchy rises before our eyes.

What an awful vitality is here! What a heavenly-sustained sovereignty! What a self-evident divinity! She claims, she seeks, she desires no temporal power, no secular station; she meddles not with Cæsar or the things of Cæsar; she obeys him in his place, but she is independent of him. Her strength is in her God; her rule is over the souls of men; her glory is in their willing subjection and loving loyalty. She hopes and fears nothing from the world; it made her not, nor can it destroy her. She can benefit it largely, but she does not force herself upon it. She may be persecuted by it, but she thrives under the persecution. She may be ignored, she may be silenced and thrown into a corner, but she is thought of the more. Calumniate her, and her influence grows; ridicule her—she does but smile upon you more awfully and persuasively. What will you do with her, ye sons of men, if you will not love her, if at least you will not endure her? Let the last three hundred years reply. Let her alone, refrain from her; for if her counsel or her work be of men, it will come to nought; but if it be of God, ye cannot overthrow it, lest perhaps you be found even to fight against God.

And here I might well stop, for I have brought the line of thought which I have been pursuing to an end; but it is right to inquire how our enemies view these things, as well as how we view them ourselves; and this will lead me to ask your patient attention for a longer time.

PART II.

Et videntes eum super mare ambulantem, turbati sunt, dicentes, Quia phantasma est. Et præ timore clamaverunt.

And they, seeing Him walking upon the sea, were troubled, saying, It is an apparition. And they cried out for fear.

Yes, my dear Brethren, would I could end at the point to which I have brought you! I ought to be able to end here; it is hard I cannot end here. Surely I have set before you a character of the Church of this day remarkable enough to attach to her the prerogatives of that divinely favoured bark in which Peter rowed, and into which the Eternal Lord entered, on the lake of Genesareth. Her fortunes during eighteen centuries have more than answered to the instance of that miraculous protection which was manifested in the fisher's boat in Galilee. It is hard that I must say more, but not strange; not strange, my Brethren, for both our Saviour's own history and His express word prepare us to expect that what is in itself so miraculous would fail to subdue, nay, would harden, the hearts of those to whom it so forcibly appeals.

There is, indeed, no argument so strong but the wilful ingenuity of man is able to evade or retort it; and what happens to us in this day happened to Him also, who is in all things our archetype and forerunner. There was a time when He wrought a miracle to convince the incredulous, but they had their ready explanation to destroy its cogency. "There was offered unto Him," says the Evangelist, "one possessed with a devil, both blind and dumb; and He healed him, so that he both spoke and saw. And all the multitudes were amazed, and said, Is not this the son of David? But the Pharisees hearing it, said, *This man casteth not out devils but by Beelzebub, the prince of the devils.*" So said the Pharisees; and He of whom they spoke forewarned His disciples, that both He and His adversaries would have their respective representatives in after times, both in uttering and bearing a like blasphemy. "The disciple is not above his master," He said, "nor the servant above his lord. It is enough for the disciple that he is as his master, and the servant as his lord. *If they have called the goodman of the house Beelzebub, how much more them of His household!*"

So it was, my Brethren, that our Saviour was not allowed to point to His miracles as His warrant, but was thought the worse of for them; and it cannot startle us that we too have to suffer the like in our day. The Sinless was called Beelzebub, much more His sinful servants. And what happened to Him then, is our protection as well as our warning now: for that must be a poor argument, which is available, not only against us, but against Him. For this reason, I am not called upon to enter upon any formal refutation of this charge against us; yet it will not be without profit to trace its operation, and that I shall now proceed to do.

The world, then, witnesses, scrutinizes, and confesses the marvellousness of the Church's power. It does not deny that she is special, awful, nay, supernatural in her history; that she does what unaided man cannot do. It discerns and recognizes her abidingness, her unchangeableness, her imperturbability, her ever youthful vigour, the elasticity of her movements, the consistency and harmony of her teaching, the persuasiveness of her claims. It confesses, I say, that she is a supernatural phenomenon; but it makes short work with such a confession, viewed as an argument for submitting to her, for it ascribes the miracle which it beholds, to Satan, not to God.

This being taken for granted, as an initial assumption from which the whole course of investigation is to proceed, and to which every result is to be referred,—viz. that the Church is not the spouse of Christ, but the child of the evil one, the sorceress described by St. John; and her supreme head, not the vicar of Christ, and pastor and doctor of His people, but the man of sin, and the destined deceiver and son of perdition,—I say, this being assumed without proof on starting, it is plain that the very evidences, which really demonstrate our divine origin, are plausibly retorted on us, as they were retorted on our Lord and Saviour, as tokens of our reprobation. Antichrist, when he comes, will be an imitative or counterfeit Christ; therefore he will *look* like Christ to the many, otherwise he would not *be* a counterfeit; but if Antichrist looks like Christ, Christ, of course, must look like Antichrist. The idolatrous sorceress, if she is to have any success in her enchantments, must feign a gravity, an authority, a sanctity, and a nobleness, which really belong to the Church of Christ alone; no wonder, then, since Satan is to be able to persuade men that she is like the Church, he is also able to persuade them that the Church is like her. Christ Himself twice was not recognized even by His disciples in the boat, who loved Him: St. Peter did not know Him after the resurrection, till St. John detected Him; and when, before this, He came walking on the sea, they at first were afraid of Him, as though He had been some evil or malignant being: "they were troubled, saying,

It is an apparition, and they cried out for fear." No wonder the enemy of souls should have abundant opportunity and means of seducing the thoughtless and the headstrong, when the very Apostles, in the first years of their discipleship, were so dull in spiritual apprehension.

1. I say, the more numerous and striking are the evidences of the divinity of the Church, so much the more conclusively are they retorted against her, when men assume at starting that she comes, not from above, but from below. Does she claim to be sent from God? but Antichrist will claim it too. Do men bow before her, "and lick up the dust of her feet"? but on the other hand, it is said of the Apocalyptic sorceress also, that the kings of the earth shall be made "drunk with her wine." Does the Church receive the homage of "the islands, and the ships of the sea"? The answer is ready; for it is expressly said in Scripture that the evil woman shall make "the merchants of the earth rich by the abundance of her delicacies." Is the Church honoured with "the gold and frankincense of Saba, the multitude of camels, the dromedaries of Madian, and the flocks of Cedar"? Her impious rival, too, will be clothed "in purple and scarlet, and gilded with gold," and enriched with "beasts, and sheep, and horses, and chariots." Does the Church exercise a power over

the soul? The enchantress, too, will be possessed, not only of the goods of this world, but of "the souls of men." Was it promised to the sons of the Church to do miracles? Antichrist is to do "lying wonders." Do they exhibit a meekness and a firmness most admirable, a marvellous self-denial, a fervency in prayer, and a charity? It is answered: "This only makes them more dangerous. Do you not know that Satan can transform himself into an angel of light?" Are they, according to our Lord's bidding, like sheep, defenceless and patient? This does but fulfil a remarkable prophecy, it is retorted; for the second beast, which came up out of the earth, "had two horns like a lamb's, while it spoke as a dragon." Does the Church fulfil the Scripture description of being weak and yet strong, of conquering by yielding, of having nothing yet gaining all things, and of exercising power without wealth or station? This wonderful fact, which ought surely to startle the most obstinate, is assigned, not to the power of God, but to some political art or conspiracy. Angels walk the earth in vain; to the gross prejudice of the multitude their coming and going is the secret plotting, as they call it, of "monks and Jesuits." Good forsooth it cannot, shall not be; rather believe anything than that it comes from God; believe in a host of invisible traitors prowling about and disseminating doctrine adverse to your own, believe us to be liars and deceivers, men of blood, ministers of hell, rather than turn your minds, by way of solving the problem, to the possibility of our being what we say we are, the children and servants of the true Church. There never was a more successful artifice than this, which the author of evil has devised against his Maker, that God's work is not God's but his own. He has spread this abroad in the world, as thieves in a crowd escape by giving the alarm; and men, in their simplicity, run away from Christ as if Christ were he, and run into his arms as if he were Christ.

2. And if Satan can so well avail himself even of the gifts and glories of the Church, it is not wonderful that he can be skilful also in his exhibition and use of those offences and scandals which are his own work in her now or in former times. My Brethren, she has scandals, she has a reproach, she has a shame; no Catholic will deny it. She has ever had the reproach and shame of being the mother of children unworthy of her. She has good children;—she has many more bad. Such is the will of God, as declared from the beginning. He might have formed a pure Church; but He has expressly predicted that the cockle, sown by the enemy, shall remain with the wheat, even to the harvest at the end of the world. He pronounced that His Church

should be like a fisher's net, gathering of every kind, and not examined till the evening. Nay, more than this, He declared that the bad and imperfect should far surpass the good. "Many are called," He said, "but few are chosen"; and His Apostle speaks of "a remnant saved according to the election of grace." There is ever, then, an abundance of materials in the lives and the histories of Catholics, ready to the use of those opponents who, starting with the notion that the Holy Church is the work of the devil, wish to have some corroboration of their leading idea. Her very prerogative gives special opportunity for it; I mean, that she is the Church of all lands and of all times. If there was a Judas among the Apostles, and a Nicholas among the deacons, why should we be surprised that in the course of eighteen hundred years, there should be flagrant instances of cruelty, of unfaithfulness, of hypocrisy, or of profligacy, and that not only in the Catholic people, but in high places, in royal palaces, in bishops' households, nay, in the seat of St. Peter itself? Why need it surprise, if in barbarous ages, or in ages of luxury, there have been bishops, or abbots, or priests, who have forgotten themselves and their God, and served the world or the flesh, and have perished in that evil service? What triumph is it, though in a long line of between two and three hundred popes, amid martyrs, confessors, doctors, sage rulers, and loving fathers of their people, one, or two, or three are found who fulfil the Lord's description of the wicked servant who began "to strike the manservants and maidservants, and to eat and drink and be drunk"? What will come of it, though we grant that at this time or that, here or there, mistakes in policy, or ill-advised measures, or timidity, or vacillation in action, or secular maxims, or inhumanity, or narrowness of mind have seemed to influence the Church's action or her bearing towards her children? I can only say that, taking man as he is, it would be a miracle were such offences altogether absent from her history. Consider what it is to be left to oneself and one's conscience, without others' judgment on what we do, which at times is the case with all men; consider what it is to have easy opportunities of sinning; and then cast the first stone at churchmen who have abused their freedom from control or independence of criticism. My Brethren, with such considerations before me, I do not wonder that these scandals take place; which, of course, are the greater in proportion as the field on which they are found is larger and wider, and the more shocking in proportion as the profession of sanctity, under which they exhibit themselves, is more prominent. What religious body can compare with us in duration or in extent? There are crimes enough to be found in the members of all denominations: if there are passages in our history, the like of which do not occur in the annals of Wesleyanism or of Independency, or the other religions of the day, recollect there have been no Anabaptist pontiffs, no Methodist kings, no Congregational monasteries, no Quaker populations. Let the tenets of Irving or Swedenborg spread, as they never can, through the world, and we should see if, amid the wealth, and power, and station which would accrue to their holders, they would bear their faculties more meekly than Catholics have done.

Come, my Brethren, I will use a very homely illustration; suffer it, if it be but apposite. You know what a sensation railway accidents occasion. Why? because so enormous are the physical and mechanical forces which are put in motion in that mode of travelling, that, if an accident occurs, it must be gigantic. It is horrible from the conditions under which it takes place. In consequence; it impresses the imagination beyond what the reason can warrant; so that you may fall in with persons, who, on hearing, and much more, on undergoing such a misfortune, are not slow to protest that they never will travel by a railroad again. But sober men submit the matter to a more exact investigation. They do not suffer their minds to be fastened down or carried away by the thought of one or two casualties which shock them. They consider the number of lines, the frequency of trains, the multitude of passengers; they have recourse to the returns, and they calculate the average of accidents, and determine the percentage. And then they contrast with the results thus obtained the corresponding results which coach travelling supplies, and they end, perhaps, by coming to the conclusion that, in matter of fact, the rail is safer than the road; and yet still, in spite of these undeniable facts, there are timid persons, whose imagination is more active than their reason, and who are so arrested by the exceptions, few as they are, that they cannot get themselves to contemplate the rule. In consequence they protest as steadily as before, that steam travelling is perilous and suicidal, and that they never will travel except by coach. Oh, my Brethren, there are many such alarmists in religion; they dress out in tract or pamphlet, they cut out and frame, some special story of tyranny, or fraud, or immorality in the long history of world-wide Catholicism, and that to them is simply Catholicism,—that to them is nothing short of a picture, a definition of Catholicism. They shrink from the great road of travel which God has appointed, and they run, as I may say, their own private conveyance, be it Wesleyanism, or

Anglicanism, or Dissent, on their own track, as safer, surer, pleasanter, than the Catholic way of passage, because that passage is not secure from danger and mishap. And if this frame of mind is possible in a matter of this life, into which prejudice, and especially religious prejudice, does not enter, much more commonly and fatally will it obtain, when men are not looking for reasons to ascertain a point, but for arguments to defend it.

3. You see, my Brethren, from what I have been saying, how it is that on the one hand, the visible prerogatives of Catholicism do but make men suspicious of it, while on the other its scandals are sure to fill them with dread and horror. But now let me pursue the matter further; let me attempt to trace out more fully how the English mind, in these last centuries, has come to think there is nothing good in that Religion, which it once thought the very teaching of the Most High. Consider, then, this: most men, by nature, dislike labour and trouble; if they labour, as they are obliged to do, they do so *because* they are obliged. They exert themselves under a stimulus or excitement, and just as long as it lasts. Thus they labour for their daily bread, for their families, or for some temporal object which they desire; but they do not take on them the trouble of doing so without some such motive cause. Hence,

in religious matters, having no urgent appetite after truth, or desire to please God, or fear of the consequences of displeasing Him, or detestation of sin, they take what comes, they form their notions at random, they are moulded passively from without, and this is what is commonly meant by "private judgment." "Private judgment" commonly means passive impression. Most men in this country like opinions to be brought to them, rather than to be at the pains to go out and seek for them. They like to be waited on, they like to be consulted for, they like to be their own centre. As great men have their slaves or their body servants for every need of the day, so, in an age like this, when every one reads and has a voice in public matters, it is indispensable that they should have persons to provide them with their ideas, the clothing of their mind, and that of the best fashion. Hence the extreme influence of periodical publications at this day, quarterly, monthly, or daily; these teach the multitude of men what to think and what to say. And thus it is that, in this age, every one is, intellectually, a sort of absolute king, though his realm is confined to himself or to his family; for at least he can think and say, though he cannot do, what he will, and that with no trouble at all, because he has plenty of intellectual servants to wait on him. Is it to be supposed that a man is to take the trouble of finding out truth himself, when he can pay for it? So his only object is to have cheap knowledge; that he may have his views of revelation, and dogma, and policy, and conduct,—in short of right and wrong,—ready to hand, as he has his tablecloth laid for his breakfast, and the materials provided for the meal. Thus it is, then, that the English mind grows up into its existing character. There are nations naturally so formed for speculation, that individuals, almost as they eat and drink and work, will originate doctrines and follow out ideas; they, too, of course, have their own difficulties in submitting to the Church, but such is not the Englishman. He is in his own way the creature of circumstances; he is bent on action, but as to opinion, he takes what comes, only he bargains not to be teased or troubled about it. He gets his opinions anyhow, some from the nursery, some at school, some from the world, and has a zeal for them, because they are his own. Other men, at least, exercise a judgment upon them, and prove them by a rule. He does not care to do so, but he takes them as he finds them, whether they fit together or not, and makes light of the incongruity, and thinks it a proof of common sense, good sense, strong shrewd sense, to do so. All he cares for is, that he should not be put to rights; of that he is jealous enough. He is satisfied to walk about, dressed just as he is. As opinions come, so they must stay with him: and, as he does not like trouble in his acquisition of them, so he resents criticism in his use.

When, then, the awful form of Catholicism, of which he has already heard so much good and so much evil—so much evil which revolts him, so much good which amazes and troubles him—when this great vision, which hitherto he has known from books and from rumour, but not by sight and hearing, presents itself before him, it finds in him a very different being from the simple Anglo-Saxon to whom it originally came. It finds in him a being, not of rude nature, but of formed habits, averse to change and resentful of interference; a being who looks hard at it, and repudiates and loathes it, first of all, because, if listened to, it would give him much trouble. He wishes to be let alone; but here is a teaching which purports to be revealed, which would mould his mind on new ideas, which he has to learn, and which, if he cannot learn thoroughly, he must borrow from strangers. The very notion of a theology or a ritual frightens and oppresses him; it is a yoke, because it makes religion difficult, not easy. There is enough of labour in learning matters of this life, without concerning oneself with the revelations of another. He does not choose to believe that the Almighty has told us so many things, and he readily listens to any person or argument maintaining the negative. And, moreover, he resents the idea of interference itself; "an Englishman's house is his castle"; a maxim most salutary in politics, most dangerous in moral conduct. He cannot bear the thought of not having a will of his own, or an opinion of his own, on any given subject of inquiry, whatever it be. It is intolerable, as he considers, not to be able, on the most awful and difficult of subjects, to think for oneself; it is an insult to be told that God has spoken and superseded investigation.

4. And, further still, consider this: strange as it may be to those who do not know him, he really believes in that accidental collection of tenets, of which I have been speaking; habit has made it all natural to him, and he takes it for granted; he thinks his own view of things as clear as day, and every other view irrational and ludicrous. In good faith and in sincerity of heart, he thinks the Englishman knows more about God's dealings with men, than any one else; and he measures all things in heaven and earth by the floating opinions which have been drifted into his mind. And especially is he satisfied and sure of his *principles;* he conceives them to be the dictates of the simplest and most absolute sense, and it does not occur to him for a moment, that objective truth claims to be sought, and a revealed

doctrine requires to be ascertained. He himself is the ultimate sanction and appellate authority of all that he holds. Putting aside, then, the indignation which, under these circumstances, he naturally feels in being invited to go to school again, his present opinions are an effectual bar to his ever recognizing the divine mission of Catholicism; for he criticizes Catholicism simply by those opinions themselves which are antagonists of it, and takes his notes of truth and error from a source which is already committed against it. And thus you see that frequent occurrence, of really worthy persons unable to reconcile their minds, do what they will, to the teaching and the ways of the Catholic Church. The more they see of her members, the more their worst suspicions are confirmed. They did not wish, they say, to believe the popular notions of her anti-Christian character; but, really, after what they have seen of her authorities and her people, nothing is left to them but an hostility to her, which they are loth to adopt. They wish to think the best of every one; but this ecclesiastical measure ·, that speech, that book, those persons, those expressions, that line of thought, those realized results, all tend one way, and force them to unlearn a charitableness which is as pernicious as it is illusory. Thus, my Brethren, they speak; alas, they do not see that they are assuming the very point in dispute; for the original question is, whether Catholics or they are right in their respective principles and views, and to decide it merely by what is habitual to themselves is to exercise the double office of accuser and judge. Yet multitudes, of sober and serious minds and well-regulated lives, look out upon the Catholic Church, and shrink back again from her presence, on no better reasons than these. They cannot endure her; their whole being revolts from her; she leaves, as they speak, a bad taste in their mouths; all is so novel, so strange, so unlike what is familiar to them, so unlike the Anglican prayer-book, so unlike some favourite author of their own, so different from what they would do or say themselves, requires so much explanation, is so strained and unnatural, so unreal and extravagant, so unquiet, nay, so disingenuous, so unfeeling, that they cannot even tolerate it. The Mass is so difficult to follow, and we say prayers so very quickly, and we sit when we should stand, and we talk so freely when we should be reserved, and we keep Sunday so differently from them, and we have such notions of our own about marriage and celibacy, and we approve of vows, and we class virtues and sins on so unreasonable a standard; these and a thousand such details are, in the case of numbers, decisive proofs that we deserve the hard names which are heaped on us by the world.

5. Recollect, too, my Brethren, that a great part of the actions of every day, when narrowly looked into, are neither good nor bad in themselves, but only in relation to the persons who do them, and the circumstances or motives under which they are done. There are actions, indeed, which no circumstances can alter; which, at all times, and in all places, are duties or sins. Veracity, purity, are always virtues— blasphemy, always a sin; but to speak against another, for instance, is not always detraction, and swearing is not always taking God's name in vain. What is right in one person, may be wrong in another; and hence the various opinions which are formed of public men, who, for the most part, cannot be truly judged, except with a knowledge of their principles, characters, and motives. Here is another source of misrepresenting the Church and her servants; much of what they do admits both of a good interpretation and a bad; and when the world, as I have supposed, starts with the hypothesis that we are hypocrites or tyrants, that we are unscrupulous, crafty, and profane, it is easy to see how the very same actions which it would extol in its friends, it will unhesitatingly condemn in the instance of the objects of its hatred or suspicion. When men live in their own world, in

their own habits and ways of thought, as I have been describing, they contract, not only a narrowness, but what may be called a one-sidedness of mind. They do not judge of us by the rules they apply to the conduct of themselves and each other; what they praise or allow in those they admire is an offence to them in us. Day by day, then, as it passes, furnishes, as a matter of course, a series of charges against us, simply because it furnishes a succession of our sayings and doings. Whatever we do, whatever we do not do, is a demonstration against us. Do we argue? men are surprised at our insolence or effrontery; are we silent? we are underhand and deep. Do we appeal to the law? it is in order to evade it; do we obey the Church? it is a sign of our disloyalty. Do we state our pretensions? we blaspheme; do we conceal them? we are liars and hypocrites. Do we display the pomp of our ceremonial, and the habits of our Religious? our presumption has become intolerable; do we put them aside and dress as others? we are ashamed of being seen, and skulk about as conspirators. Did a Catholic priest cherish doubts of his faith? it would be an interesting and touching fact, suitable for public meetings; does a Protestant minister, on the other hand, doubt of the Protestant opinions? he is but dishonestly eating the bread of the Establishment. Does a Protestant exclude Catholic books from his house? he is a good father and master; does a Catholic do the same with Protestant tracts? he is afraid of the light. Protestants may ridicule a portion of our Scriptures under the name of the Apocrypha: we may not denounce the mere Protestant translation of the Bible. Protestants are to glory in their obedience to their ecclesiastical head; we may not be faithful to ours. A Protestant layman may determine and propound all by himself the terms of salvation; we are bigots and despots, if we do but proclaim what a thousand years have sanctioned. The Catholic is insidious, when the Protestant is prudent; the Protestant frank and honest, when the Catholic is rash or profane. Not a word that we say, not a deed that we do, but is viewed in the medium of that one idea, by the light of that one prejudice, which our enemies cherish concerning us; not a word or a deed but is grafted on the original assumption that we certainly come from below, and are the servants of Antichrist.

6. Now, my dear Brethren, I have not said a word of much more that might be insisted on, and of the greatest importance. I have not said a word of the unhappy interest that men have in denying a Religion so severe against the wilful sinner as ours is:—no one likes a prophet of evil. Nor have I shown you, as I might, how natural it is, that they who sit

at home and judge of all things by their personal experience of what is possible, and their private notion of what is good, should, humanly speaking, be incapable of faith in religious mysteries, such as ours. They think nothing true which is strange to them; and, in consequence, they consider our very doctrines a simple refutation of our claims. Nor, again, have I spoken of the misrepresentations and slanders with which the father of lies floods the popular mind, and which are so safe to utter, because they are, as he knows, so welcome to hear. Alas! there is no calumny too gross for the credulity of our countrymen, no imputation on us so monstrous which they will not drink up greedily like water. There is a demand for such fabrications, and there is a consequent supply; our antiquity, our vastness, our strangeness, our successes, our unmovableness, all require a solution; and the impostor is hailed as a prophet, who will extemporize against us some tale of blood, and the orator as an evangelist, who points to some real scandal of the Church, dead and gone, man or measure, as the pattern fact of Catholicism. And thus it comes to pass that we are distrusted, feared, hated, and ridiculed, whichever way we look; all parties, the most hostile to each other, are still more hostile to us, and will combine in attacking us. No one but is brave enough to spurn us; it is no cowardice to accuse us when we cannot answer, no cruelty to fasten on us what we detest. We are fair game for all comers. Other men they view and oppose in their doctrines, but us they oppose in our persons; we are thought morally and individually corrupt, we have not even natural goodness; we are not merely ignorant of the new birth, but are signed and sealed as the ministers of the evil one. We have his mark on our foreheads. That we are living beings with human hearts and keen feelings, is not conceived; no, the best we can expect is to be treated as shadows of the past, names a thousand miles away, abstractions, commonplaces, historical figures, or dramatic properties, waste ground on which any load of abuse may be shot, the convenient conductors of a distempered political atmosphere, who are not Englishmen, who have not the right of citizens, nor any claim for redress, nor any plea for indulgence, but who are well off, forsooth, if they are allowed so much as to pollute this free soil with their odious presence.

And thus we are thrown back on ourselves: for nothing we can do on the stage of the world, but is turned against us as an offence. Our most innocent actions, our attempts to please the community, our sanguine expectations of conciliating our foes, our expressions of love, are flung back upon us with scorn, to our pain and disappointment. Our simplicity, inexperience of life, ignorance of human nature, or want of tact and prudence, are put down to duplicity; and the more honest and frank are our avowals, the more certainly it is thought that a fraud lurks in the background. We are never so double-dealing as when we are candid. We are never so deep as when we have been accused and acquitted. Thus we find ourselves quite at fault how anything we do is likely to be taken; and at length, with wounded feelings, we determine to let it alone, as never knowing where to find men, or how to treat them. I have often been reminded, my Brethren, by these circumstances of ours, of the complication, not uncommon, I think, in the fictions of a popular writer who died some twenty years ago. He delights to represent innocent persons involved in circumstances which plausibly convict them of guilt, and which they are unable satisfactorily to explain. I think I recollect a young man who is accused of treason, and who, when fact after fact is brought forward to his disadvantage, conscious of his innocence, yet feeling the ingenuity of the allegation, and the speciousness of the evidence by which it is supported, and, moreover, the prejudice and cold suspicion of his judge, bursts into tears, buries his head in his hands, and refuses to answer any more interrogatories. "Do your worst," he seems to say, "not a word more shall you extract from me. You refuse to believe me; cease to question me. You are determined I am guilty; make the most of your persuasion." What is there represented in fiction happens to us in fact. We are innocent, we seem guilty, we despair of the vindication which we deserve; but we do not bury our faces in our hands, we raise our hands and our faces to our Redeemer. "As the eyes of servants are on the hands of their masters, and the eyes of the handmaid are on the hands of her mistress, so are our eyes unto the Lord our God, until He have mercy upon us. Have mercy on us, O Lord; have mercy on us, for we are greatly filled with contempt. We are a reproach to the rich and a contempt to the proud." To Thee do we appeal, O true Judge, for Thou seest us. We care not for man while we have Thee. We can afford to part with the creature while we have the Creator. We can endure "the snare of an unjust tongue, and the lips of them that forge lies," while we have Thy presence in our assemblies, and Thy witness and Thy approval in our hearts.

We do not, then, we cannot, rejoice in a mere worldly temper or in a political tone, on occasion of the event which we are celebrating to-day: no, we are too conscious both of our divine prerogatives and our high destiny, and again of the weight of that calumny and reproach which is our cross. We rejoice, not "as those who rejoice in the harvest, or as conquerors rejoice when they divide the spoils." We rejoice surely, but solemnly, religiously, courageously, as the priests of the Lord when they were carrying into battle "the ark of the Lord, the God of the whole earth." We rejoice, as those who love men's souls so well that they would go through much to save them, yet love God more, and find the full reward of all disappointments in Him; as those whose work lies with sinners, but whose portion is with the saints. We love you, O men of this generation, but we fear you not. Understand well and lay it to heart, that we will do the work of God and fulfil our mission, with your consent, if we can get it, but in spite of you, if we cannot. You cannot touch us except in a way of which you do not dream, by the arm of force; nor do we dream of asking for more than that which the Apostle claimed, freedom of speech, "an open door," which, through God's grace, will be "evident," though there be "many adversaries." We do but wish to subdue you by appeals to your reason and to your heart; give us but a fair field and due time, and we hope to gain our point. I do not say that we shall gain it in this generation; I do not say we shall gain it without our own suffering; but we look on to the future, and we do not look at ourselves. As to ourselves, the world has long ago done its worst against us: long ago has it seasoned us for this encounter. In the way of obloquy and ridicule it has exhausted upon us long since all it had to pour, and now it is resourceless. More it cannot say against us than it has said already. We have parted company with it for many years; we have long chosen our portion with the old faith once delivered to the saints, and we have intimately comprehended that a penalty is attached to the profession. No one proclaims the truth to a deceived world, but will be treated himself as a deceiver. We know our place and our fortunes: to give a witness, and to be reviled; to be cast out as evil, and to succeed. Such is the law which the Lord of all has annexed to the promulgation of the truth: its preachers suffer, but its cause prevails. Joyfully have we become a party to this bargain; and as we have resigned ourselves to the price, so we intend, by God's aid, to claim the compensation.

Fear not, therefore, dear Brethren of the household of faith, any trouble that may come upon us, or upon you, if trouble be God's will; trouble will but prove the simplicity of our and your devotion to Him. When our Lord walked on the sea, Peter went out to meet Him, and, "seeing the wind strong he was afraid." Doubt not that He, who caught the disciple by the hand, will appear to rescue you; doubt not that He, who could tread the billows so securely, can self-sustained bear any weight your weakness throws upon Him, and can be your immovable refuge and home amid the tossing and tumult of the storm. The waves roared round the Apostle, they could do nothing more: they could but excite his fear; they could but assault his faith; they could not hurt him but by tempting him; they could not overcome him except through himself. While he was true to himself, he was safe; when he feared and doubted, he began to sink. So it is now: "your adversary, the devil, as a roaring lion, goeth about:" it is all he can do. So says the great Saint Antony, the first monk, who lived his long life in the Egyptian desert, and had abundant experience of conflicts with the evil one. He tells his children that bad spirits make a noise and clatter, and shout and roar, because they have nothing else to do; it is their way of driving us from our Saviour. Let us be true to ourselves, and the blustering wind will drop, the furious sea will calm. No, I fear not, my Brethren, this momentary clamour of our foe: I fear not this great people, among whom we dwell, of whose blood we come, and who have still, under the habits of these later centuries, the rudiments of that faith by which, in the beginning, they were new-born to God: who still, despite the loss of heavenly gifts, retain the love of justice, manly bearing, and tenderness of heart, which Gregory saw in their very faces. I have no fear about our Holy Father, whose sincerity of affection towards his ancient flock, whose simplicity and truthfulness I know full well. I have no fear about the zeal of the college of our bishops, the sanctity of the body of our clergy, or the inward perfection of our Religious. One thing alone I fear. I fear the presence of sin in the midst of us. My Brethren, the success of the Church lies not with pope, or bishops, or priests, or monks; it rests with yourselves. If the present mercies of God come to nought, it will be because sin has undone them. The drunkard, the blasphemer, the unjust dealer, the profligate liver,—these will be our ruin; the open scandal, the secret sin known only to God, these form the devil's real host. We can conquer every foe but these: corruption, hollowness, neglect of mercies, deadness of heart, worldliness,—these will be too much for us.

And, O my dear Brethren, if, through God's mercy, you are among those who are shielded from these more palpable dangers and more ordinary temptations of humanity, then go on to pray for all who are in a like state with yourselves, that we may all "forget the things that are behind, and stretch forth to those that are before"; that we may "join with faith, virtue, and with virtue, knowledge, and with knowledge, abstinence, and with abstinence, patience, and with patience, pity, and with pity, love of brotherhood, and with love of brotherhood, charity." Pray that we may not come short of that destiny to which God calls us; that we may be visited by His effectual grace, enabling us to break the bonds of lukewarmness and sloth, to command our will, to rule our actions through the day, to grow continually in devotion and fervour of spirit, and, while our natural vigour decays, to feel that keener energy which comes from heaven.

BACKGROUND

It is difficult now to imagine the condition of Catholics in the England of 1850 when, after three hundred years, the Catholic hierarchy was restored. Catholicism was reckoned an alien thing, unworthy of free-born Englishmen, full of superstition and tyranny and the suppression of free enquiry and intellectual dignity: the vehicle of Antichrist. Newman eloquently outlines this situation, and argues that it is no more than a Christian should expect: this was what was promised to the first disciples. Yet we, like Peter, are called to step out of the boat and walk towards Christ: so we should know that our fears, like his, are groundless. Jesus will take our hand and keep us safe; at his word, the storm will cease and the waters fall.

Today, we may not recognise the situation that Newman saw in 1850; but it does not take much imagination to apply what he said then, to the surely analogous challenges Catholics face now.

CTS ONEFIFTIES

1. FR DAMIEN & WHERE ALL ROADS LEAD • *Robert Louis Stevenson & G K Chesterton*
2. THE UNENDING CONFLICT • *Hilaire Belloc*
3. CHRIST UPON THE WATERS • *John Henry Newman*
4. DEATH & RESURRECTION • *Leonard Cheshire VC & Bede Jarrett OP*
5. THE DAY THE BOMB FELL • *Johannes Siemes SJ & Bruce Kent*
6. MIRACLES • *Ronald Knox*
7. A CITY SET ON A HILL • *Robert Hugh Benson*
8. FINDING THE WAY BACK • *Francis Ripley*
9. THE GUNPOWDER PLOT • *Herbert Thurston SJ*
10. NUNS – WHAT ARE THEY FOR? • *Maria Boulding OSB, Bruno Webb OSB & Jean Cardinal Daniélou SJ*
11. ISLAM, BRITAIN & THE GOSPEL • *John Coonan, William Burridge & John Wijngaards*
12. STORIES OF THE GREAT WAR • *Eileen Boland*
13. LIFE WITHIN US • *Caryll Houselander, Delia Smith & Herbert Fincham*
14. INSIDE COMMUNISM • *Douglas Hyde*
15. COURTSHIP: SOME PRACTICAL ADVICE • *Anon, Hubert McEvoy SJ, Tony Kirwin & Malcolm Brennan*
16. RESURRECTION • *Vincent McNabb OP & B C Butler OSB*
17. TWO CONVERSION STORIES • *James Britten & Ronald Knox*
18. MEDIEVAL CHRISTIANITY • *Christopher Dawson*
19. A LIBRARY OF TALES – VOL 1 • *Lady Herbert of Lea*
20. A LIBRARY OF TALES – VOL 2 • *Eveline Cole & E Kielty*
21. WAR AT HOME AND AT THE FRONT • *"A Chaplain" & Mrs Blundell of Crosby*
22. THE CHURCH & THE MODERN AGE • *Christopher Hollis*
23. THE PRAYER OF ST THÉRÈSE OF LISIEUX • *Vernon Johnson*
24. THE PROBLEM OF EVIL • *Martin D'Arcy SJ*
25. WHO IS ST JOSEPH? • *Herbert Cardinal Vaughan*